A DEEPER FEAR
OF
REPENTANCE

PERRY DOUGLAS SISK

A DEEPER FEAR OF REPENTANCE

Copyright © 2024 by Perry Douglas Sisk

All rights reserved. No part of this publication may be reproduced, distributed, or transmitted in any form or by any means, including photocopying, recording, or other electronic or mechanical methods, without the prior written permission of the copyright owner and the publisher, except in the case of brief quotations embodied in critical reviews and certain other noncommercial uses permitted by copyright law. For permission requests,write to the publisher, addressed "Attention: Permissions Coordinator," at the address below.

CITIOFBOOKS, INC.
3736 Eubank NE Suite A1
Albuquerque, NM 87111-3579
www.citiofbooks.com
Hotline 1 (877) 389-2759
Fax: 1 (505) 930-7244

Ordering Information:
Quantity sales. Special discounts are available on quantity purchases by corporations, associations, and others. For details, contact the publisher at the address above.

Printed in the United States of America.

ISBN-13:	Softcover	979-8-89391-228-9
	eBook	979-8-89391-229-6

Library of Congress Control Number: 2024915345

A Deeper Fear of Repentance

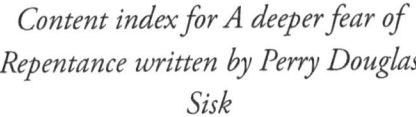

Content index for A deeper fear of Repentance written by Perry Douglas Sisk

1--A dream held over
2--One color of living
3--For sake of one direction
4-- These words most fail to mention
5--For all he had cried
6--These souls we bear
7--The son we will find again
8--Moving on
9--What the spirit sees
10--Much the same
11--One angel's faith as well

Perry Douglas Sisk

12--Unity and praise
13--What is to know
14 -- Never alone--no date given
15--No truth is ever hidden
16--Consider if
17--A cost for time
18--I Am here
19--A will mend
20--A reason kept at heart
21-- Why a child shall lead
22--With home we help to share
23--Free will | sing
24--Where truth remains
25--Instruction handed down

A Deeper Fear of Repentance

26--Better words to read
N
27--A face led time
28--Set apart but not alone
29--The father's call
30--A door yet to open
31-- I love that come to mind
32--A gift that has always been
33--One reason to hold
34--Some that fail to hear
35--A time to outlast
36--The few that hold
37--Finding hope
38--A tide so turned
39--This time so near

Perry Douglas Sisk

40--Red set apart
41--Lastly heard
42--Patience to know
43--True faith to lead
44--A better ending
45--First or last
46--Ending true
47--The end of a vision
48--A season to return
49--That trumpet heard
50--Sight within
51--Run of time
52--Lean on truth
53--Trust no fear

A Deeper Fear of Repentance

54--One priceless soul
55--His creation never fades
56--One song never written
57--Only the father to know

Perry Douglas Sisk

A dream held over- - Perry Sisk - - 24 Feb 24
A purpose for a dream comes to mind to ask again
To shine a light on things that's been
Even though there are gadgets that do the same
Those toys that man create with pointed finger hold the shame
To hold that balance that is seen so rare in hearts that picture there
As still as captured within one stare
Are dreams given man be reminders of Simply
lll-fated events that spell out why they
Lost at love succinctly
These days we live out seem pointless to an end
Though shadows in our dreams tell our story or just how to spend
This all too brief and shorter time we
Share with those we've lost yet still we hope we bare
Remembrance of that path we took to walk again a closer look
As was like a reel of film captured frame by frame won't hide
Contempt or Envy for some or all as humans hold inside
Of those dreams we won't dispel to any whom we face
Out of fear or ridicule or simple lack of Grace
If indeed our lives are measured counted Deeds by God above
Dreams alone won't hide from him were filled with hate or love,,,,,,
1

A Deeper Fear of Repentance

One color of living
Perry D Sisk - - Feb 24
Don't you ever ask yourself why everyone's blood is red,
Even fish and deer or steer we see
Along with Martha Mabel and Ted,
Funny is that that some will spat over things themselves will show
Why dwell on things as commonplace
Get on with yourself now go,
I guess as it were | will always infer
To others in the crowd
Yet some will argue please get to the point
What purpose was raised allowed
Is it always true to Nature that we tend to speculate
To find a better ending or ever knowing the fact or fate
So simple | see one remedy for all the trials we face
When given free will from day one did we spill
Here what marks this human race
Just as in those words he had said to always be depicted in red
1

Perry Douglas Sisk

Stands out for any to see
From the time of Genesis and now to you and me
This answer so plain instead
The color of his life he shed ....

A Deeper Fear of Repentance

For sake of One Direction ——Perry Sisk - - - 16 Feb 24
These things we as humans share
Should never stain the fabric or even cause to tare
That part of each and all that possess
A sense to know or care,
Indeed, there was a time I thought
I could climb that highest mountain alone
And doing so and until then though
I find ambition gone
Then does come a time that those dreams I had thought were mine
I discovered not so rare
So now to realize these things I see with older eyes
From Simply sitting in this chair
This time I take to merely contemplate on those years I took for granted
At this stage as I turn another page
Of a vision that was oh so slanted
Thus, I say to one and all that did ever take the fall
Given time it turns around
So, to ask where we are going all this while
We still are never knowing which is truly sound

Perry Douglas Sisk

All those measures taken within our dreams that left us shaken
Did did we see just where we are going
That One Direction knowing,...

A Deeper Fear of Repentance

These words mast fail to mention
Some have said it before
many will say it again
From that one and only time of beginin
There is only one thats been
Able to teach not always to preach
those paths that we should walk
wiiile some will resist
and always persist
in harshness some did talk
So many thoughts thot they knew well
at times as i did too
See purpose for all he spoke
Though too that class
like broken glass
in pain what words invoke
With darkened skies
amidst their cries
the anger they did stoke

Perry Douglas Sisk

There will be ones
that spoke in many tongues
never hearing whats been said
For that lock of understanding
and for all they were demanding
That day who's blood was she
Never saw that cross he carried
up that hill
where all had tarried
saw not the blood he'd spill
All true justice thot was failed
on thot cross of which
was nailed
our redemption he had shown
those lost three words he'd spoken
His gnger was then woken
he said that it was done
Perry d sisk--jan 024

A Deeper Fear of Repentance

For ali he had cried
Perry d sisk--Jan 024
Something to ask
What will anything of this world
ever do for you
when this world passes away and replaced
by one thats new
For all this life consists of
is simply passage of time
never wonder of no other reason
be so qouted here in ryhme
To find one single purpose
we are put here in this place
to see what holds out longest
Ones passion for the race
if ever intervention be so needed
be devine
All those seeking retrobution
1'd be first to stand in line
One thing thats absoclute they say

Perry Douglas Sisk

His word speaks of the day
We are alf fallen short of true salvation
for truly only one will say
Your name i see is written here
so welcome come on in
For those he'li say he never knew
that never asked to remove my Sin
For where i've been and things i've done
is fairly cut and dried
For all who lives he still forgives
even though for all he died
Thus, i know his Son had cried

A Deeper Fear of Repentance

These Souls we bare - - Perry Douglas Sisk -. - 17 February 24
All these things | see now that are coming to fruition
Just tend to lend a truer relevance to one's better intuition,
For once there was a time even though my years, they were not many
Something given me away to see was more to some or any,
Would see an end result to things
Before or far removed
To find one's place | still would Chase those dreams I'd share ensued,
Onward in time as if to stand in fine
Hand-picked for things to come
Not holding a voice was nor given by choice out of so many or by some
While | get feeling captured by those being raptured
At a time that no one knows
This isolation of the flesh that gave Credence to this mesh
Of Spirited ones that goes
Back to the start where we are sent from God's heart
In this we base our souls ...,,,..

Perry Douglas Sisk

The son we will find again - - Perry Douglas Sisk - - 20 Feb 24
In bygone days we would often say don't speak till spoken to
Now it seems these Newfound ways cause hardship to ensue,
When everybody is knowing just where everybody is going
Let alone they're goings on
One would have to ask just how much
There would be to go so wrong,
Do we not have to wonder just when we took the turn
That leads us off the righteous path
Onto that one that will burn,
Speaking for myself there are things best left upon the Shelf
To gather dust and leave alone
Those things that break the heart and further calls to fall apart
To all we then atone,
As I'm sure that there are days that many mistake my ways
To speak my thoughts aloud
How else does one extend to those that do pretend
They'd Stand Out amidst a crowd,
Some strive to walk the path laid out from day one
As well as getting lost amidst the clouds of adversity
They still will find again the Son

-

A Deeper Fear of Repentance

Moving on - - Perry D Sisk ---
Time in this life on Earth and experience needed
For when we pass on into another Journey
Yet unseen still yet be heeded
All the many chastisements or all those smaller accounts of praise
Are these the steppingstones that bring
A spirit upon we gaze,
Our sites are focused high above
To the heaven's lights at night, we love
Seek we are fulfillment or purpose for just being met
So, nothing here this path no stone is ever set
This stage we're on today and tomorrow
What gives us joy or paints Us in sorrow
We all go forward moving on -,, -

Perry Douglas Sisk

What the spirit see's
Perry Douglas Sisk, '+ February 024
Where has gone now we ask that once known
Cohesion we thought was meant to last,
That glue that holds together our hearts our souls and
Minds
Call it substance or call it will
This reason for Humanity and those who seldom find,
So many are those sorted perceptions that paint a picture
wrong
As the palate of an artist missing colors
That would otherwise be used as strong
Those blacks and Browns and greens below
To show our lands beneath
With blues and grays and whites astray
Of clouds that float a wreath
While those that view this world from afar and all that
indeed, it holds

A Deeper Fear of Repentance

Forget with time that very sign
A love profound and bold
Silence is said to be the absence of sound
Therefore, blindness must be what's in sight never found
All things hold a purpose and reasons for being
That glue that keeps together
What our spirit keeps seeing ', ,...

Perry Douglas Sisk

Much the same - - p d Sisk - - Feb 24
Well again | Rise from on all two brief amounts of slumber
Feeling like I'd stacked away A Long flatbed of lumber,
Now | guess one would ask ain't there never no sense in knowing
That the older we all get with that
The time we rest so downward Now is slowing,
am | down just a might with every passing day
Yet still we dream of a time we all did play
As kids after dark at the creek or in the woods
For you see back then there wasn't much to do
cep't be told just who was bad and who did hold the goods
Or so it goes and Heaven Knows those games as kids we played
Now looking back no time to lack
those days we'd wish we stayed
And that time so innocent and rare by contrast today
S0 few we find would care
Onward through some years that would be deemed as bitter or Sweet

A Deeper Fear of Repentance

One Angel's Faith as well ---Perry d Sisk--November 022
There may be up high a windowsill where Angels sit in heaven
Often counted twelve or so with one less sits 11,
They gaze out through a windowpane upon this Earth to see
Who it is that stands the most one visit meant for thee 5
If it is true they indeed do walk with only but a few
They single out with utmost doubt of who they always knew.
For in this mix of souls they fix who sought so far away
Those most that count and higher number do they pick a given day,
Short-lived it seems by those with dreams they can't recall in full
As one puzzle piece the effort ceased one corner piece will rule
A portrait whole that hides the soul distressed by lack of vision
I hope to gain one better train of thought or solid stood decision,
Except a gift so meant to lift that Spirit seen of one
Angelic being spent time and seeing his task will so be done,

1

That shout some call one Angel to fall to Earth and rescue one
That kept their faith in the one and only son
Angels Faith as well did run...,,,

A Deeper Fear of Repentance

Unity and praise----Perry Douglas Sisk--December 022
As though it's been scripted few lives ever lifted by efforts of Their Own
It takes many days to get through the haze of Misdeeds their fortunes had shown,
Some lack the luster or Sheen they could muster as due to failed endeavor
Along with a cluster of clouds raining Bluster that seem to last forever,
The only in one day to all that see with dismay
That broader path to walk
Those always cast in all the wrong light
Leaves no more said or talk
Are we not granted still those many blessings ignored at will
Confronted with a truth be told desires of the heart will not fulfill
To be cast as modest and humbled more
Lends some to open or close a door
That Stir of emotion with voice and song
Give him praise and hold it long

Perry Douglas Sisk

For what is evidenced every hour that we breathe is this
One devout conclusion ever left or so is missed
What we see and what we hear every single day
The beauty of a smile on the face of a child at play
The power God gives a voice to sing a note so high the Angels ring
In one Accord we praise our Lord his glory all to bring---... Okay

A Deeper Fear of Repentance

What is to know - --- Perry d Sisk--January - 021
On this day while added thoughts did come to mind
Some folks I've met that never care or even think to be so kind,
Another Eve | watched the sunset slowly in the West
As it's fading rays that glimmer on Waters of a lake they slowly come to rest,
Now with failed recognition of the life as passing by
That lack of wisdom in early years now finds a graying brow above an eye,
Those who fall in love too soon while placing dreams upon the Moon
Soon find they too with cause to complain from early on and well past noon
Some Revel in the Deeds they feel were good they had done
And some will dispute and not Proclaim that God was indeed his son
When all is said and done, and all is laid so bare

1

Perry Douglas Sisk

Who will be left to evidence one spirit always there
So many will not know just what to say or do
Yet will there be those singled out referred to as the few that knew
What's to know-------.....

A Deeper Fear of Repentance

True Faith to lead---Perry Sisk---September 023
Well again here we are and yet have things gone so far
As some will raise and lower the bar
Though while looking up at night, we find
One shining brighter star
Do we yet wonder what chance this was
And the short span of life we miss
Were we not left with one written guide
Throughout this course of time, we slide
One truth so often we do so overlook
Those words written in red all to often we mistook
Looking closer it will reveal
That life Everlasting is nothing we can steal
Earned not by Deeds or Works performed
In with what is real
And Injustice found of bitter scorn
Bow our heads fall on our knees

Perry Douglas Sisk

Hands raised High the spirit sees
What's not of this world but pastures Beyond
Those Meadows and streams one Golden Pond
Friends and family waiting there
The love contained in memory to share
Look not behind nor gaze to the Past
Keep our sight forward in faith to outlast
Instructions received we hope and believe
A truth found through faith
As his word did perceive
And ability to see
Those things we cannot touch
To not question what is real
Was never too much
This trust not so blindly given
By words that we do read
One truth in his word in faith it will follow
Our faith in him shall lead................

A better ending---Perry Sisk---25 September 023
To say that in our life we all make choices
as the painter paints his pictures
And the singers used their voices
Some will say you cannot bend facts
And certain issues are a given
Though hope to find a truth among lies
As one Spirit dies among the living
Never knowing being redeemed or rewarded
For what ignorance of Youth
And the wrongs that you had courted
Turning a blind eye and a deaf ear to your guidance
As time did progress still found no reliance
Well it may take a very long journey to reveal mistakes made
Only in summer will a tree offer shade

Perry Douglas Sisk

When Seasons no longer discern one to the other
Where then was | allowed
To be the keeper of my brother
For in due course of time
All things are brought to light
All this while a race to an end
A better end in sight.............

A Deeper Fear of Repentance

First or last ' PERRY DOUGLAS SISK----26
SEPTEMBER 023
HERE AM | TO WITNESS
THE LEAST OF FOUR GETTING ON AN AGE
NOW IS A TIME TO PONDER
WHICH OF US WILL BE FIRST TO LEAVE THE STAGE
BORN TO A GROUP OF SIBLINGS THREE
THOSE THINGS THEY OUTGREW HANDED DOWN TO ME
THAT TIME LONG AGO FAR AWAY AND IN OUR PAST
COMMON GOODS HARD TO COME BY
AS THE RAIN IN THE DESERT FADES AWAY ALL TOO FAST
LIKIN TO THESE YEARS LOOKED WE BACK UPON AND NOw
SO MISS THOSE DAYS OUR FOLKS DID USE
A COMMON HORSE AND PLOW

Perry Douglas Sisk

THIS LIFE WE'VE LIVED AS A PLAY ON A STAGE CALLED
LIVING
BEING THIS FORTH OUT OF FOUR
WHO WAS LACKING WHO WAS GIVING
WILL IT GO WITHOUT SAYING AS | WATCH JUST WHICH
DEPARTS
KNOWING ALL TOO WELL
THAT THIS MUST BREAK ALL OUR HEARTS
THE ONLY SOLACE THAT CAN BE FOUND
IN KNOWING WHAT MUST BE
THIS FAITH IN A BETTER HEREAFTER THAT BRINGS
US ALL TOGETHER AGAIN
HERE BE ALL WE HOPE TO SEE
WILL IT BE ME---.........

A Deeper Fear of Repentance

ENDING TRUE-------- PERRY SISK--10 OCTOBER 023
WHEN THE MYSTERY OF A DREAM IS ALL WE HAVE LEFT
PEOPLE WE ONCE KNEW COME BACK
AND HAUNTING WAYS THE TWO HAVE DEPARTED WEST
WHAT IS TO SAY ETERNITY HAS A DIRECTION
WHO COMMITS TO KNOW THAT POINT OF INSURRECTION
THIS FIGHT BETWEEN GOOD AND EVIL
HAS LONG SINCE BEEN KNOWN
BY EVERY MAN AND WOMAN BEFORE
THEIR PARENTS AS WELL THEIR SEEDS THEY HAD SOWN
ARE THERE NOT TIMES WE WISH TO BE A CHILD AGAIN
WITH THAT OUTSTRETCHED PATH OF LIFE TO ONCE AGAIN
BEGIN
LONG HAS IT BEEN SAID THERE IS NOTHING WAYWARD
WORSE
THAN LOOKING BACK ON WHAT WAS DONE
NOT BEING ABLE TO CHANGE IS MUCH MORE THAN ONCE
CURSE
CHARACTERS EVOLVED WITH EACH AND EVERY PASSING
YEAR
THOSE SEASONS OF OUR YOUTH TO SEE

Perry Douglas Sisk

THAT LACK OF WISDOM AND STILL ONE MEASURED FEAR
BEAR WITNESS | TO SO MANY SEEMINGLY LOST
WITHIN AN ARROGANCE OR PRIDE
GIVING NO RELEVANCE TO A COST
YET TO BE PAID OR EVEN PAST APPRAISED
LEFT NOW TO INSPECT OR EVER WONDER JUST
HOW SO MANY OF US WERE RAISED
NOT IN SO MUCH THOSE VALUES INSTILLED
OR WERE THEY EVER PASSED ON DOWN
SO EASY DO WE OFTEN INTERPRET
WHY ONE FACIAL EXPRESSION TURNS TO A FROWN
ALL WE BETTER JUDGED FOR GIVING OF ONESELF
OR CALL IT A MISPLACED VIRTUE
FOR IN THAT ALONE WE FIND OURSELVES
WITH ALL LAID BARE TO KNOW JUST WHAT IS
TRUE..................

A Deeper Fear of Repentance

I am here--Perry Sisk -,-December 023
And yet another Christmas Has Come Around again
Where those months far to this time did go so fast can anyone guess but then
We know it happens every year and all the course of season
The fact this holiday falls at end of year could hold one certain reason
To look to and honor a father and his son
In looking on this past year's time to recall what good was done
As | sit here in the silence and this Stillness of my home
Be reminded giving thanks and praise unto his name so known
Giving purpose to the joy of spirit spreads to all
Lends us to ask on that day of judgment who did answer to his call
To celebrate the birth of our Lord is the highest treasured gift for all of One Accord
And that and in this season once per year should hold that solemn truth our Lord says plainly do not fear | am here........

Perry Douglas Sisk

A will to mend---Perry Sisk--January 024
In dwelling on one subject matter that leaves one so elated
I must confess confused am | convinced also persuaded
To believe all things have purpose for thanks taken too long to show
Given in time exceptions find one's illuminated glow
We see Among Us them that know just why or what to reason
Ways to fix a troubled heart throughout each and every season
Those who weep for just one lost sheep will spread the word
when found
Told to be still and regain the will to again be safe and sound
Sound of spirit and Mindless Wonder to know what dreams can hold
So solution for to know what door to open we once were told
Told to believe in things we don't see wherein is found one's fate
To hold to Heart what speaks of a truth that love overpowers hate
From that day we are born all weather a storm this life alone
predicts

A Deeper Fear of Repentance

A reason kept at heart,, -- Perry D Sisk--May 023
Raising thought to things present day
There is in this summation one has to say
It seems inherent as shown many times
This Repeat Performance that crosses the line
Regardless when issued be proved in a fact
The topic discussed seems always to lack
One common cycle two double triple down
On answers to questions in fact are found sound
It seems that in every facet of being
Their lives one purpose to convince a majority so leaning
A one and stated remedy seems never be kept in hand
In a solution found whatever placed in sand
Always given way to sway or tilt its Purpose By Design
Never left alone and just accept that truth we find
This all to human need to show just where truth and fact will go
As is the essence of a freshly fallen snow
Given the climate it is here one moment and gone the next
Should anyone ask why are we so perplexed
That power to hold Once Fashion for ransom

1

Perry Douglas Sisk

As did Delilah cut the hair from the head of Mighty Samson
Truer to this point when seen for what it is
To curb the pain this acid so brings the potion for it will fizz
All things that arise we see with our eyes we should know there is more we don't
See for what we are told is how fast by the cold that nature sometimes it won't
Bring us to focus on those who are chosen
To fall so set apart with that gumption that know full consumption
A reason kept at heart------

A Deeper Fear of Repentance

This day I was awakened by a whisper in my ear
To rise and shine and offer thanks for a brand new
day and not one touch of fear
If I could lend a voice which could travel across this land
Not stopping at the shores or stalled at Desert Sand, I
Would ask to Every Nation all those with sense to hear
Had we not been told as children of those Mansions way up high
Not one would shed a tear
There will be no pain or even strife ushered in this everlasting life
For this I know a promised kept so written in a book
Not one single eye that wept refused to even look
Should I be granted just one wish I dare to ever tell
That everyone upon this world recapture what once we held
The Innocence not to sell
Why a child shall lead ---Perry Douglas Sisk - - 3 April 23

Perry Douglas Sisk

3/3/2024
With home we hope to share - - Perry Douglas Sisk - - 26 Feb 24
Now having reached this ripe old age of 67,
Ever more so today I'd wish to go back and Be just 10 or 11
Countless others have said the same I'm sure just as any illness known
Sometimes better than it's cure,
At times the so-called side effects of living day to day
As they fly in the ointment the elders used to say,
We'll call it wise to hear of life through older eyes
Taking note of apprehensions when we hear their heavy sighs,
Prompted by the knowledge of some things they wish they'd done
Still with hope of better change with each New Rising Sun,
Whosoever betrays their inner convictions
So often end up with stricter restrictions,
If 1 could paint a picture to Forever look upon
It would be a family forever living on,
Be it here or be it where we still won't know just when
Iust so long as God's love shines and keeps us all with him ......

A Deeper Fear of Repentance

Free Will I sing - - Perry d Sisk - - 7 May 23
Reflections of the Skies on Waters reveal elusive dreams
Inspired unto our sons and daughters
A love so hoped for seems
Profound their care so sought for there
So seldom ever found
In time to spare those feelings where
To never voice a sound
What fondness do we feel for what is otherwise
found so real,, is what we cannot work around
Or to ever find a seal
Things that take us back,, a song a fragrance
A dream we remember a coin we found
Also simple it seems all to be
Those issues coming back to you and me
With such beauty in this world we look past every day
1 answer to 1 question never will we see or say
Gone unnoticed through decades past
And even centuries long His glory and his praise
For God voiced in a song
Free Will being right never seeing what was wrong ,,,,,,,

Perry Douglas Sisk

" *What was that old saying grow old with me*
the best jg yetto be, or does there come a point to
rather say there's just not much more to see,,
3_.39.:@ not what reflections ¢ame upon those We chose as brothers,
These thoughts my friend must not offend
though more will 50 declare
First to Seek that Kingdom of GOD,
for truth wjjj always pe found there.....
WHERE TRUTH REMAINS--....._. Perry Douglas Sisk---14 feh 024

A Deeper Fear of Repentance

Instruction handed down ---Perry Sisk--03-Jan-023
I was reminded of what lies | had spoken
That sense of Shame for being one's token
Used and abused for evil sake
And ignorance of what there was such at stake
Being given this hand held tour of a life
At times at ease and so often with strife
Those steps | took without thinking through
Good or bad who could say they ever knew
This Angel sent for indeed he was
Sent from prayer as everyone does
He went on to show my Deeds | committed
Those that were cherished some blemished with truth omitted
To bring to a Forefront it's never too late
While still | am living to alter my fate
This purpose alone was | gifted this gift
To some intervention to allow and to lift
Those scales from my eyes this life had allowed

Perry Douglas Sisk

To see in full force two doors through a cloud
One opens to that life that | had wasted
The other | knew of though yet to be tasted
Pick one or the other it's still up to me
He stated with a smile then know where he was
Was this all real or in part just a dream
That allowed me to see a life yet unseen-------......

A Deeper Fear of Repentance

Better words to read-----Perry Sisk---December 023
Something more to voice and take note of
This all too short span of Living For The Love
When I hear folks talk about having been a great many years
So many fail to ever mention who did count the tears
Was it ever more truly said that man upstairs
Took time to count upon our head the hairs
I'm sure that he had never missed
The tears on mother's cheek I'm sure the angel kissed
That chased away that fear and anguish
As her labor saw we wouldn't languish
Such as the shame it's taken this long to understand
Her love was never written in a song
Those precious times that we now miss
Too many lines to ever list
Take it to heart we will come to know
Though all those Joys will come and go
Not given True Justice for What it all stood to show

Perry Douglas Sisk

Those many nights we walk the floor
That one that knocked and came into
Hopes to see there at the door
That one that knocked and came on in
The Peace of Mind he promised when
Will live on Evermore
Those words that Jesus spoke and said
Those words laid out in crimson red
Are all we should read instead--------————..........

A Deeper Fear of Repentance

A face in time-----Perry Sisk---December 023
Again | find myself in a reflective frame of mind
While I'm sitting in this Stillness so often hard to find
I've tried to recall just when the motion of life grew faster
That pace of pages calendar turns for most would spell disaster
For in as much and losing touch what did past years hold within
That time frame of each said meant to teach get as much done as we can
Isn't it strange that when we're young the sand on a beach seem endless
Not giving thought to where we stand as in a game of chess
If memory serves the point | remember was 40 + or so
From then and on the Tempo of a song was such that | should know
Granted these days will pass in the haze a cloudy Misty vision
Put to a tune not meant to impure this time holds with precision
If life for a fabric and time was the Stitch that holds it all in place
What fortunes we spend to try and yet Bend the hands of time now race
Each day we will find deeper our lines reflected on our face--------------
....

Perry Douglas Sisk

Set apart but not alone----Perry Sisk---December 023
You know more and more I'm seeing clear
Though my vision is dim
These Soul felt passions of Life draw near
Years past they seem so slim
They say that to dwell on things that take you down
Leaves more in the face
Than a somber frown
Those lows and highs we felt every day
Though Sundays that | missed
Where people pray
I never held to being in a way a crowd pleaser
Keeping to myself | thought was all the more so easier
All that's left of my family still today
are just my three siblings that live too far away
| told myself many long years ago

A Deeper Fear of Repentance

Some friends | have that live close by and lordy ain't it so
All brought about by my own hand | guess
But being far from home where would | be laid to rest
As most will have it I'd end up where | started
Never Letting be ever seen this life | led partly
Brokenhearted
Here again no wants to blame
This world | did not tame
This test called life it all ends the same--------

Perry Douglas Sisk

The father's call-----Perry Sisk--02 March 024
Is there nothing oh so precious
That will last for but a while
Than when we see that angel of a baby
Around 2 months or so will smile
| think that is why our father sends them down
To keep us smiling too and replace that worried frown
Charcoal as with all manner of folk be they rich or be they poor
That one and single constant is that new dads will walk the floor
And anticipation of what God sends down
What new face to look upon
If a boy he hopes will follow in his ways
Or even a daughter whose love for him it stays
For either or one can't ignore
This purpose hidden there
As we grow old and given time to rock them in our chair
Sooner than not with time they got much wiser all too fast
Putting aside what we all will hide of Dreams we keep of past

A Deeper Fear of Repentance

Past and back on a time we could not see that Wonder of it all
Call it what you will this true nature even still
Have we all walked down that Hall
That Hall that simply leads
God had placed those seeds
Of Love he makes the call--------

Perry Douglas Sisk

A door yet to open----Perry Sisk---December 023
One Night in a dream being awoken from I've seen
A taller figure standing there beside my bedroom chair
As if to tell me come take a seat
And he said don't put no house shoes on your feet
Not knowing or question who this was
I kind of just took for granted or was it just because
Then this being standing there
Now along my side while in my chair
Gave subtle gentle voiced instruction
To close my eyes | gave no obstruction
What seemed to me been just one moment
I look toward this being wearing white and glowing garment
Emitted the brightness of the Sun
Then I knew there is only one
He said we will now take a journey past
Those Seasons that were and those forecast
In this moment I could feel where I sat all the joys
And all the Sorrows coming back
With all the wicked ploys

A Deeper Fear of Repentance

I had to ask why show me this
He said be silent or | will miss
This reason being singled out
This way leaves Little Wonder
And never little doubt
A door yet left to open----------

Perry Douglas Sisk

I love that come to mind——Perry Sisk---January 024
1 day I found myself and seemingly heavy thought
Of people once I knew back when
My thoughts were few of learning those friendships bought
in youth we steal a pride we feel much later seen not earned
Those highs and lows of the time that shows
those years had justly burned
With Souls encased and bodies made of clay and dust of Earth
Returning back from where we came that very day of birth
Some believe upon reprieve our spirit unseen takes flight
To join with others not seen by day are counted for by night
For could it be that you and me were destined toward that sky
Our spirit it takes it's place in this case
In a twinkle of his eye
Every night God pulls the shade on the light that he had made
Giving rest to those that toil
As it rains upon the soil
What life will grow we find for his love we keep in mind

A Deeper Fear of Repentance

A gift that has always been----Perry Sisk--January 024
From humble beginnings we strive to gain a spark
And along up to that point to say we'd made our mark
Whether in service to one another
Or a love to embrace our brother
Giving a chance we call our own
that 1 day said that it was shown
Gifts are often hidden and wrapped in different many a shade
Too late though are they shared with years
And thus they fade
Only held Immortal by way of memory
and never lose their given time they left for history
Breaking the hold that the braids of constraint what's woven tight they're
on
Confined to Darkness others did place to say their talents gone
Deceived by some Unearthed by 1 would lend to share a dawn
Brought to light what was the plight a resisted lyrical song
With words in place that easily Trace to Origins rare yet near

Perry Douglas Sisk

The many who lend an ear to hear dissects a given tone
Will soon Discover it was never another
Comes so readily said in stone............

A Deeper Fear of Repentance

One reason to hold---Perry Sisk

I often Venture back to the days that time just seemed to crawl
As an injured Cricket found trapped in the house does cling along the wall
Those days we were young the hours that were strung
End to end within the day
Hesitate though bare the wait
For night we hit the hay
With chores to do we still were made to see then through
Upon which made us glad
That end of the day and still though too looking back on makes us sad
In looking onward and yet unseen
gives cause for trepidation that few of us could glean
All of those tell tale signs said the writings on the wall
Were not for all those Brave that indeed withstood a fall
Where it not for past mistakes
Did we choose for all our sakes
To wait and watch as time sped fast
We could not help but see
All those hopes we would Outlast and some still yet to be
All those memories of a child

Perry Douglas Sisk

Some we cherish some abhor
Serve to provide never to hide a purpose we all ignore
For all who hold a bitter past in part amidst their Joy
In later years find talents for just where one could employ
Now see we calls to take and pause and look on where we placed
That strength of will that God has passed those trials with which we all were faced
To know that higher purpose for all we saw then clear
One place in time revealed the sign
of who we keep and hold so near...........

A Deeper Fear of Repentance

Some that fail to hear ---Perry Sisk--March 024
Now that I have gotten older
I am all the more convinced
There surely are and must have been
More cause for recompense
As with so many of my age
With memory that stands alone
All the deeds and favors done
For good or bad atone
Of course as memories fade
And dreams become obscure
Just as summer bring trees their shade
Through Seasons they will endure
Never Let It Go unsaid
What has been put to bed

Perry Douglas Sisk

That tried and true devotion
That keeps in mind hold those so kind
With ones own isolation
If we all were to be appraised
On what standards we were raised
Giving credit where it's due
Those Generations past with their principles that last
Are carried out on just a few
Further safe to say with my hair now thin and gray
Can | picture what's to come
It's the wise who seek repentance
While the fool will serve a sentence
Great will be that number
That Miss while in their slumber
That trumpet heard by some.............

A Deeper Fear of Repentance

A time to outlast -- Perry Sisk--December 023
For those that live will past their days
They do so in many obscure and Elusive ways
It has been said that some will live on
if only in the memories of those
Who have yet to be gone
But failure being pointed out to all
That hold one premise
Those songs those books those plays in theater
Often overlooked and remiss
Give we attention to detail
For what all will leave behind
To even out a score
That one true measure of compassion
That most won't boast or be known for

Perry Douglas Sisk

Those singled out that had held a proper stance
Done so from a fear of some
Held to their losing chance
To one day held in higher regard
For the better traits they showed
Never being at any time aware
Of the inner truth so barred
By indignation of Burden towed
Thus being made Immortal in those ways that all Revere
These thoughts here in should be observed
For those we shall always keep so near......

A Deeper Fear of Repentance

The few that hold----Perry Sisk--December 023
Something more I feel we should observe
In every generation we see few that been the Curve
There are those that are gifted with high IQ
And also some that remain alone
And hidden we soon would wish we knew
For them who hold a talent for
The benefit of good
So often misperceived for things of which they stood
In my life of modest and meager Association
1 know that \ have met with some of higher aspiration
Although in all too many cases
These types who should stand tall
To be given admiration for their fight to scale a wall
That wall of achievement too few give credit for

Perry Douglas Sisk

Foresight of faulty reason
They are seldom given more
Attention for how they were formed
That no one can Define
Outside the single fact to say
Brought forth by God's design
So never take for granted
those we meet and fail to seek
Those made of special fiber
That were placed among the weak
They say there is strength in numbers
For the most part this is true
Never should we pass on by
That chance to one day know
For some may well be hidden angels
Placed among us too

A Deeper Fear of Repentance

That hold a gift and talent rare
From God they soon do always show
His powers within a few..........

Perry Douglas Sisk

Finding hope--Perry Sisk--November 023
In time there Comes A Time to evaluate was their reason
Being of concern for what is real
we survive for seeing every season
Was there ever one single purpose found
First simply giving cause to be
For countless years we find this same
Event revealed we see
In this life we are brought to being
For growth allows the heartache flee
Words they filter through a subtle Summer Breeze
As thoughts brought to mind amidst the winds that blow
Conclusion few will know though brought about withease

A Deeper Fear of Repentance

To all the questions ever asked
Given time that few will know
Though many upheavals across our world
There does reside one course
Ever marching forward never back to truly know a source
For this I find a glimpse of peace of Mind
That stems from absolution
All things that begin will soon sooner end
With absolute Revolution
Forecasting rain upon the plain does bear a fruitless task
why proceed at loss concede
To know when not to ask
Where resides Our Hope..........

Perry Douglas Sisk

A tide so turned--Perry Sisk--March 023
Today we see what times we're in
that thing called social media set to spend,,
People's lives through washing cycle
These many to wonder what's next to rival,,
This catchphrase of today
tossed to and fro By Word of Mouth
What we witness is laid out in Scripture
To all four corners North and South
These folks that preach today
Show a world is downside up
While some will wonder what are we drinking
From what cup
Those that go as far to say

A Deeper Fear of Repentance

To have our come to Jesus moment
And pray
For back and long ago had we heard it said
Just wait there will come a day
Voicing for myself it's true
In some ways early on | knew
We best give God his Praises High
That first path to wisdom
To fear Mighty God his son draws nigh
So none should fear for who draws near
Be humbile in spirit with hope to abide
The Father's love everlasting will forever turn the

Perry Douglas Sisk

This time so near—-Perry Sisk —-April 023
Ever will they be
A story one day told
How one far-reaching Generation
Were stood its own demise so cold
Notwithstanding this current
chapter of History will show
This fight of evil and good
Has been in place written records know
Being said today there has never been a time
So much a bitter divide to reveal how prevalent this
decline
Those that say we have been here before
And always saw it through
Failed to note we wear this coat

A Deeper Fear of Repentance

God's armor protects us too
All this talk of end times we preach
Through morning noon and night
This Doom and Gloom so constant spread
In darkness though we still will find the light
One path so seen as night becomes day
We're told to choose a side
Of a wall so tall to breach this tied to fear
Behind of which we hide
For righteousness sake one choice to make
Becomes ever more so clear
All God's chosen instilled with faith
His son Will Keep Us near...........

Perry Douglas Sisk

Red set apart-----Perry Sisk---April 023
As reflection comes about some say
It looks as though we've lost our way
When Shadows follow those lead astray
Walk to one light let go of decay
Mistakes of our past our present or future
Depending vastly on a knowledge known for sure
While tolerance of so many we rarely get to know
Carried burdens lightly for fear of letting go
One judgment falls on but a few
Though will Encompass everyone who knew
To strive to right those wrongs committed

A Deeper Fear of Repentance

Failing to address all those omitted
Some will serve there is no clear path ahead
Those that hold the mark
Will tow the line instead
Shall we all shall we all take heed
Those words he wrote and red.........

Perry Douglas Sisk

Lastly heard----Perry Sisk---30 June 023
When man sees our Lord as obsolete
With Saints and Angels gathered at his feet
Humanities arrogance and haughty ways
Once warm now cold and elegance sways
Will there ever come a time all knowing were remiss
For ever seeing well one joyfulness or Bliss
As years stack upon each other
With a wisdom never found
Long we for the day that utterance of Peace will sound
One ponderance looking on and back
What Legacy Humanity would be noted for
Those many wrongs with lesser rights
Substituting fear for a reason they ignore

A Deeper Fear of Repentance

With End of Days the end of time
Being spoken all around
So much this noise drowns out one message
Of Hope and Faith profound.........

Perry Douglas Sisk

Patience to know---Perry Sisk
What is it that compels
The human being to survive
What is this Breath of Life God put
Into His Image to always stay alive
When will | be called home
after time has left
Nowhere else | choose to roam
That scar upon my chest
How will | be sent back
From where this journey started
A happiness when life did lack
Some see as Brokenhearted
To pick and choose what more to lose
Or ever Ponder will
As Waters upon this Lake of life

A Deeper Fear of Repentance

This early morning kept still
With Kindred Souls past through time it Folds
I'd seek one Brighter Day
To once again find solace in those known
That once had passed my way
We will share once more
As times before so pure a fallen snow
One reason for being
One purpose for living
Well past our time we will know.................

Perry Douglas Sisk

Never alone -- Perry d Sisk - no date given
What will be passed along to who that will wear my shoes
For who will better sing the song best sang in classic Blues
Some may find early on in life who they are meant to be
Before the tragic loss of their child or a wife don't you see
What things such as this and the absence of that kiss
He used to find at his door forever more to miss
This thing we call one's character that we know takes time to
build None in so much that Golden Touch or a heart that's passion
filled For those that labor long and hard to reach one proper end
Though all the while maintain one style that some can never
Bend What is better to ever be known for in this life so brief
That measure of the way those who run are those that stay to
handle their own grief
Once portrayed as that wreath is laid within the shadow of a
1

A Deeper Fear of Repentance

Stone
Never walked up to or give one mention as to who it was that went back home
For a name and a date always carved into stone only serves to address who was
Once admired by a few never known and yet too those shoes he wore because
He never walked alone------......

Perry Douglas Sisk

No truth is ever hidden--Perry Sisk--December 023
Many days and early hour morning
most times it is still sometimes it is storming
I go out into my kitchen and put some coffee on
I sit and take this pen in hand as I wait another Dawn
| see the sunrise in the east as it has for countless days
There is no getting around what peace is found in oh so many ways
Thinking back and all she said those days as a child raised in that covered shed
My grandma used to say and that older fashioned way
You'll never miss the water to the well runs dry then turn her head
Gaze up to the sky and give that heavy sigh
Giving now more thought to this leads to ponder what more to miss
Speeding faster to that day we all will soon be seeing
That in due time that Vision sign of a winged angelic being
With sight unseen | have to lean on those words for better said
Not of my own for what is now shown Where Angels Fear To Tread
Thus is true we thought we knew that path to walk was right

A Deeper Fear of Repentance

Even in Shadows this darker World holds cannot hide from his sight
For this reason this Autumn time and season
Of my time remaining do | count the days abstaining
From those | often see one truth be said to be this book | wrote Of
Me---,,,...

Perry Douglas Sisk

Consider if - Perry Sisk--August 023
I recall a time when I was 6 or 7
I think back on how my grandparents did often speak of Heaven
Of course being a kid of that age | gave no attention to words that they had spoke
I took as being old folk talk the span of my attention and being merely seven it soon enough was broke
Now as time pressed on with each and every passing Dawn
That wisdom then that passed me by comes back to me
That keeps me focused on
Giving relevance to the facts that some outlive their purpose for which intended
One should indeed find peace in knowing that soon their trials are to heed
Never however lose the site for instilled in all that will to fight
Stays present Beyond its need
This is found that hope so sound
There is more to wisdom in a word to ever really need
Giving in to those whims discounting just how Slim
We still came near that cliff
Just One Look Far Below what living did it show
We are left to consider if---.....——

A Deeper Fear of Repentance

A cost for time -- Perry Sisk --
If ever was it made clear that we live far and near
to that day of ours to reckon
In hopes there is still one less subtle fear that beckons
If ever there were an archive of time no words or
phrases could ever Define
Wherein would be determined any measure of
decline Given what we know when held to Old tradition
The older that we grow gives calls to fear perdition
Could this world and itself be just a capsule alone
That held all there has been by every counted Stone
Those that are proven to have derived from their past
One measure of thankfulness throughout their

Perry Douglas Sisk

Years Outlast
Should ever it be proven to the living or those gone
That Faith was not in vain and hope was
maintained strong
For in these words so mentioned where Faith and
Hope go forth
Keep all our aspirations his love holds Priceless

A SEASON TO RETURN----PERRY D SISK---30 MAR 024
Now that | can see this winter time frame of my life
Long ago those salad years | forget but not my wife
Things back then expected of me
Few To None would ever see
1 guess we all will write this page
Just as a job it's giving wage
That Springtime of our life did show
Just what little did we know
Moving on to Summer still
With ample strength and gifted will
That spring of Life takes place behind
What is forthcoming so willing to find
A stable home and achievements met
And yet what is more that we soon forget
The coolness of the Summer Breeze
And still we see a future set
Set in stone with choices made

Perry Douglas Sisk

Into Autumn Our Lives will fade
As coins that are tossed into a well
A tortoise hides within his shell
Fast arrived has winter came
No less to bare and still the same
That spirit that I had back in my youth
It still gives me reason though I'm long in the tooth
So be mindful of what there is to miss
Always will there be another one or this
The older that we are the less amount of time there be
Those Souls within that tree of life
Those with mine I hope to see

A Deeper Fear of Repentance

That trumpet heard------- Perry d Sisk---30 March 024
Does the good Lord move his furniture around
Or does he have some Angel do it
I have heard the thunder clap before
But this time it threw a fit
I'm sure there is much God is angry about
The shape this world is in
More regard for folks doing wrong
Then ever has there been
It sure does seem things I knew and seen
It seems so long ago
This world has now turned upside down
From all we held as sacred and true
I am sure the Lord must wear a frown
People losing sight of things that were

Perry Douglas Sisk

Once so just and right
Now we are left to wonder
If we will ever see the light
Many will be asking
What did cause this great demise
Of the land and sea and mountains
Beneath once clear and cloudless skies
Those that speak of signs and wonders
To Mark our end of days
And that wink of an eye one ending sigh
So now a trumpet plays...........

A Deeper Fear of Repentance

Sight Within-----perry d sisk--14 October 023
Why some choose to age alone
For fear of sins left to atone
If a picture holds one thousand words
I sound when sung by God's gifted Birds
There are so many thoughts to share
And yet | wonder still
Just who it is that will care
In Stillness before another Dawning light
Some find it hard resisting plight
When asked what purpose do we all hold within
I find so simple to explain again
Going back as far as anyone can know
This cause to be to age and grow
Are not the ones that stood their test of time

Perry Douglas Sisk

That saw those many uphill battles to climb
So many reached that stage they're given
Or more so they did earn
To pass down to their youngers
What parcel of wisdom they did learn
For in and around this reason
For a Seasons passed a long ones chore
Not to question why or what for
All things begin and all things end
Just as every stream and River has a Bend
One comment thread we all do share
To never justly know that when or where
We stepped from Darkness to that light
Our spirit once held inside now takes to flight
To never dismisse one gifted insight

A Deeper Fear of Repentance

Run of time------- Perry Sisk---October 023
Here again is Fall of the year
| asked what path will winter steer
While trees and grass of fields will sleep
What Shepherds stored now feeds their sheep
Long has been this pattern seen
Those grains of corn and Oak with wheat they gleen
Folk used to plan for leaner days ahead
As Seasons dictated just what
To put aside their garden toil had shed
Why has ways that used to be
Seem strange some now deny
Now only relived through a dream
And misplaced with tear of our eye
Just as a well it's water taken for granted
When empty no longer filled
Those missed opinions slanted
Now as love for neighbor's falter

Perry Douglas Sisk

The times we had compassion failing
Will love itself leave doubt
Nothing ever seen for what it truly is
For until our time Runs Out.......cccccuuunn....

A Deeper Fear of Repentance

Some things in life we must affirm
Albeit common knowledge now
Why it has taken these years to learn
The why the what and the how
Early on we struggle getting by
Seeking admonition from anyone we pass
All who look up towards the sky
A lake Serene as a Looking Glass
Though it has been said that Still Waters do Run Deep
Just as mountains we'd hope to climb
Now finding oh so steep
Those things that we see as measured
Now taking notice for
Those years we lose we hold us treasured
Who will keep the score
To be free of fear and engage a lighter frame of mind
Some find their path of lesser rage
And take hold their Kindred kind
Though there will be many who have walked

Perry Douglas Sisk

A darker Road never and always of the hope
Of not ever to be revealed or talked
Of the many that were strangled by their own rope
Not knowing just how certain those words to pick and choose
How many ever truly won
Though in the end would surely lose
Asking why one's will to survive and instilled
In every Mortal so cast into one image
This need yet ask not of love
One needless robbed and pillage
With nature often Divine or diverse
As seen in obscurity
Though relished held as sacred
Solely for its purity
Holding true that never any end will justify its means
Seen for known for and always
With adoration ones truth it Leans..........
Lean on truth---------- Perry Sisk---12 APR 024

A Deeper Fear of Repentance

Trust no fear------Perry Sisk---13 04 024
Having lived a good many years Upon This Plain
| have seen the many seasons come and go
And also at times the grief and pain
Those that paint what is said to be a glowing picture
Often use a lesser grade of paint
Thus lacking what could be richer
Summer said to be a true devout visionary
Albeit so short their time
Lacking in the knowledge
Of their dim perceptions to rhyme
Singers voice a hearts desire
Though never feeling their tone
Just as painters found in seclusion
Prefer to paint alone
For every novel ever written

Perry Douglas Sisk

The decades and centuries it end
One moral lesson said to be placed between the lines
For all to find though still so many have no will to bend oh
Throughout our lives are we not meant for change
Just as those Mustang and bison
once darkened and open range
Be still and never moving
Will cause our dreams to cease
Just as cold is of the grave
Will it ever offer peace
For through the light that God bestowed
Upon all of his creation
Therein lies that unseen warmth
Of his love from our devotion
Each and every child of God
Has hidden traits and gifts
Those seldom found in time to use
Or glorify and lift
Our hearts and Minds and hands raised High

A Deeper Fear of Repentance

With praise unto his name
Through my years dispel those fears
This world had kept the same..........c..ccec....

Perry Douglas Sisk

One Priceless soul------ Perry Sisk---11 April 024
What if we all could return to a Time
Where Grandma baked pies
Out of love not yours not mine
Suppose we'd return to a season of old
Where folks kept their hearts warm
That winter feelings unfold
Seeing one's life so stretched far and wide
A walk to a beach
Along the shore sounds of the tide
A measure of one's essence
By their fruits or their deeds
To prosper so vastly as one Spring Garden from seed
How well | recall those days in the Sun
Were accomplishment of chores
Now looked on as fun
Why harder to imagine could | go there again
Only in dreams as | sleep

A Deeper Fear of Repentance

Is where they must remain
So are they the culprit of our Spirits demise
Disguised as tools that evil uses
To Cloud our judging eyes
Dreams | mean or so it seems
Has benefits two fold
Shared by both our heart and mind
Along with young and old
Say no to the influence
We perceive to be bad
For my soul will not be sold
For has it ever been enough just to say
Yes that God has made us all from just that one lump of clay
So from that Dust We all will not evade
Thus to that beginning do we return
That Garden of Eden's shade
Where man and woman were created
That Everlasting memory of
Those as well will never fade...................

Perry Douglas Sisk

His creation never fades
Perry d Sisk--July 23 23
A picture was painted many years ago
Now is set into this Frame
So admired by young and old
Ones Journey began out of fear or remorse
This led one to wonder
What events would chart one course
One finds himself set to solitude the one did cast upon
Another view that most will look on
As lyrics we forget from an older So loved song
These days | Walk Alone
As some would find to see
Another life so set apart
From those as you and me
One has to wonder wili the arrogance and ignorance of Youth be enough
To pass muster on the day of judgment
Be eased or be it tough
Lack of fear of what's to come
For those who lack Redemption

A Deeper Fear of Repentance

Unto that day there will be those
Left without words from their hearts and their minds
Brought through to their conviction.........

Perry Douglas Sisk

One song Never written
Perry d Sisk--March 024
When life leads us down one circumstance and path
That none but if you can handle
But oh so many will grasp
Harken back to the voice that Moses heard
As when told remove your sandal
1 often believed one trait to retrieve
That was never lost or lesser than misplaced
This Light Within reveals no spin
One blood far back be traced
Inherent in all of those willing to fall
Preserving his love and peace
God gave his son
It took only one
His resurrection caused evii to cease
So upon further inspection
Though years of reflection

A Deeper Fear of Repentance

As countless talents arise
With words on paper not sooner nor later
Would be found through my demise
Was | told early on
To one day write a song
Those lyrics cast here and there
Never really knowing a pain evolved
in time that some took note to bear
If a truth ever shined
As this light cast behind
From a darkness that even Shadows hide
Those ups and downs many Smiles many frowns
Held a will to stem the tide
Letting go of a fear as an ending draws near
As the night Fades away at dawn
Up these many thoughts | choose
Hand-picked or so to lose
Were never really written for a song..........

Perry Douglas Sisk

Only the father to know
Perry d Sisk--Jan 024
If all things that are addictive
Becomes a sinful pleasure
Then why are some meant to be held close
And counted as though a treasure
Just one more of all the what ifs
To often make mention of
Question be the question none had chose
Then where does through it all does one account for love
Seems to be another Eternal mystery
That we on Earth will fail to ever see
With open eyes to endless Skies
Of night the stars if counted
A number will never be
Taken for what these lights May truly be meant for
Just to show that Majesty of design
From that day created

A Deeper Fear of Repentance

To last forever more
No one then through eons of time
Will have ever and even now defined a Justice true
Ours was never to question why
These things are as they are
No greater reality for all there is
To one known as well these simple things to him he knew
Who better to know that ebb and flow
Of time god holds in hand
That number of Souls he has collected surpass
The counted desert grains of sand
Where stars above
And earth below
in number takes the father to know..........

www.ingramcontent.com/pod-product-compliance
Lightning Source LLC
Chambersburg PA
CBHW020509030426
42337CB00011B/299